T0095662

I AM PAT

Patricia Kampmeier

Inspiring Voices®

Inspiring Voices books may be ordered through booksellers or by contacting:

Inspiring Voices
1663 Liberty Drive
Bloomington, IN 47403
www.inspiringvoices.com
1 (866) 697-5313

Cover Art: Watercolor Painting by Neva Lou Kampmeier

Scripture taken from the King James Version of the Bible.

My thanks to *Off the Coast* where "I Never Lay in Grass" was published in May 2007.

ISBN: 978-1-4624-1099-6 (e)
ISBN: 978-1-4624-1098-9 (sc)

Print information available on the last page.

Inspiring Voices rev. date: 12/9/2015

For those who have sung through me, thank you.

"Let the words of my mouth, and the meditation of my heart, be acceptable in Thy sight, O Lord, my strength, and my redeemer." Psalm 19:14 (KJV)

CONTENTS

MY NAME

Patricia is my name my name my name
And yet there is some deeper place of
    no name no name
Where the freer lighted life sings holy
    holy
And clouds cover and open and cover
    and open
And oh something is so much bigger
    than anything we can ever know
In fullness in ripeness in heady sweeter
    fruit
In grace and understanding and more
    than words or longings
And oh I live and It lives me

CONTAINING ME

The Light contains me somehow
And is me and everything
Allness of all
What was that just then that winged by
   and through me and
Changed me utterly from one to many
   and back again
Into light
And sound and colorings of such glory
   that I feel as if I have
New eyes of seeing
And dancing happens and instinctively I
   know that It is the All

FLOWER AND WEED

I am a flower and
I am a weed
I blossom flower open-wide
I also grow and infest where
I am not wanted
Where I only get in the way
Pulled up by my roots
And thrown away

CLOGGED UP

I feel tired and clogged up today
In my chest
Wish I could just release illness
Lift it off my body
So I could feel clean and free
Don't know why I'm still stuck in illness
When I'd rather be stuck in health

MAKING PANCAKES

I'm making pancakes again
Full of blueberries and walnuts
Good grains
Juicy with butter and powdered sugar

I had thought I could not cook anything
Like I used to
Mixing this and that
Together

Somehow one day
I changed my mind
Decided   decided
To try again for
Greater complexity in my meal-making

I don't know why I stopped
Why I went for many years thinking
I couldn't

I am reclaiming lost parts of myself
In this simple activity
Finding a self that once was strong
Sturdy definite

All this illness took that me away
Focused me instead somewhere else
Without that rich everyday life
Gave me another life to grow through

I really wonder who runs all this stuff
Who decides and brings into beingness
Surely I would not die to such good
Everydayness in order to live illness

It is all so strange

I guess I turned to another inner city
Than the healthy busy one I had known
So long
An inner city where my body became
Demanding of me another way of life

CAT LOVE

I miss having a cat around me in my
    home
Remember how Bootsy used to climb
    onto my lap
When I was meditating each day
And if I went away on a trip, still I
Would feel her climbing and settling on
    me anyway every day
Our spirits meeting in spite of body
    distance, I guess
She knew me then
In those quiet indrawn spaces

I miss the soft fur of Tom and Ginger
Ginger especially
With her small fine-boned girl's body
And her longer silky hair
Tom was always a solid warm weight
    on me
However he chose to curl up on me or
    near me
They each would sometimes lick my hand
Nuzzle their cool noses in my palm or
In that wedge space
Between my fingers and thumb

I spent time one week
Just watching them
Sitting quiet and looking
Looking
Ever since I have loved them mightily
Have felt their love for me
They knew I was looking
Trying to let them be wholly themselves
In their catness
And let me see them and a little bit
Know them

They each had beautiful fur
Ginger's was brown and black and grey
    and orangey,
With tabby markings
Tom's fur was black with areas of white
And he was so big.

I am sorry I only have them in memory
Sorry they have gone on to wherever
Our sweet animal companions go after
    death

ARISE AND SING

Arise, all creatures of the earth
All of earth
And sing!
Your Lord is within you
Sing for the glory of Life
Sing for the inherent possibilities
Sing for hope
Sing for sins forgiven
Sing for the exuberance of Life
Within and without

THANK YOU, GOD, FOR THE RAIN

Drink, thirsty earth!
Snails, frogs, salamanders, earthworms
Drink and wallow in joy
Splashing water
Wet skin, looser soil,
Dripping rocks
Lovely splashes into the waters of
Lake and pond and sea

Drink, all little thirsty creatures
Drink, big and little cats
Raccoons and doggies
Birdie life, drink
Drink and wallow in splashings!

Trees, plants, flowers
In pots and in the grounded soil
Hydrangeas, oleanders, cactii,
All manner of growing greens
Drink, drink!

Reservoirs, fill and flow

Smelling the wet freshness of air
Jumping in puddles
Splashing with joy as the other creatures
Splashing joy
Smelling joy
Thirsty bodies, drink!

I NEVER LAY IN GRASS

I never lay in grass
But wondered what I squished.

BLACK CLOUDS

Black clouds, black clouds
Over me
Black clouds, black clouds
Coming free

WOUNDS

Two little wounds came
From my friend today
Little sharpnesses cut
Through my warmth
Into my open heart
Sent me away

SOUR GRAPES

I'm full of sour grapes
Don't suppose I'll ever have room
For any good food again

SHUT UP! SHUT UP!

I need a flyswatter to keep him quiet!
He annoys me like a fly
Like clouds of gnats
Like mosquitoes who can't keep from
    biting me
Gaining life from my blood
My bones ache
I can't keep his noisyness
His need to judge and criticize
His top-dog needs
Away from me

Shut up! Shut up!
Keep quiet so I can be myself!

EXASPERATION

Manipulate, manipulate, manipulate!
Do you even know any other way to
 relate?!

UGLY TWISTED PLACE

I have a twisted ugly place in me
Born of dead dreams
Frustrated attempts to bring myself into
    fullness
Knowing that only when our work is
    offered to the world
Paid for
Up for public critiquing
Is it fully grown

So much I wanted not to be blocked by
    others'
Ideasandbeliefs about things
I should and shouldnotdo
How much I wanted simply to try and try
And try again to bring my own work into
    full expression
Offer it to the world for its evaluations
Others reading it and responding
Some way or another
Make it or break it

Instead it feels blocked and I will
Never know

I have a twisted ugly place in me
Where dreams die over and over again
Because of others' ideas of
What is right for me to do
Such a dark ugly hurting place

Dreams die so hard
Disappointment corroding everything
    hopeful and open
I read my work and am so moved
That something so lovely has come out
    of me, through me
I feel the value, the real life,
The depth of me
And that something Other that lives
    there
With me
I know it's good enough
I know it is right to express it
Let it come free and move outward
Into wider more open life

I feel so sad and hurt and full of longing

SOME MEN

I feel such tenderness for some men
Men who have been kind to me
Men who love children and mothers
Men who want to protect cherish value

I love them not with my sexuality
But with my heartedness
In turn want to protect and nourish them
Affirm their kindness with my
    gratefulness
Go easy on them because so much of life
    for them
Can be so hard demanding unjust scary

It is good for me to love men as I do
Not wanting to disturb their relationship
    with their wives
Not wanting to harm them in any way
Just releasing to them my tenderness
Protectiveness
Gratefulness

MEN'S CLOTHES

I like chinos and golf shirts
Plaid shirts and flannel shirts, crew neck
     tees and V-neck sweaters
Crew neck sweaters, too.

Love gray flannel suits, charcoal gray and
     oxford gray, with nice
White shirts
And splashy ties, plain ties, striped ties
Like good leather sandals, and
     Birkenstocks and loafers with no
Socks and dock shoes and even wing tips
But I don't like tasseled shoes

Like dark overcoats and hats and
     briefcases
Like a watch on a hairy arm with sleeves
     rolled up, face turned inward
Like like like
Male clothes with a nice male in them!

FRECKLES

I decided I like freckles.
He had freckles on his arms,
Very light ones, I think.

My mother had freckles.
Her skin was smooth, soft
And a nice ripe-peach color
Because of those freckles.
I liked her softness and her
Bosomy-ness
When she was older.

My sister has warm-skin
Peachy freckleness too.
I am pale, often
Too white.
I thought they were
Lucky to have been given,
Been born with, skin of
Such warmth.

And I like thinking of
His arms, the skin
On them also warm
Maybe slightly freckled,
And the way his watch was
On his wrist and
The way he turned his arm to
Look at it.

HOW IS IT POSSIBLE

I feel his shoulder and upper body in my
    mind
My cheek resting into his shoulder
I am grateful for his presence and
    comforting
However is it possible that it can be so
    real and
This time so unexpected
How much I have loved his body and
His ways of affection, comfort, sexiness

GRUMPS

You're grumpy!
Do you want me to be grumpy, too?
Too old grumps
Together might be
Better than any other
Options right now

Or I could leave you be
If you want me to

Grouchy grumpy
Yum yum
That's who my lover is!

Moods we get in.
Are you chasing me?
He says.
Yes I am, I say.
Maybe I should tickle you,
I say.
Body contact is always
Good.

I love you, my girl,
He says.
Aaahhh, that's
What I need to hear,
I say.
Making up.

My old-shoe self
Loves your old-shoe self
Without reservation.

I REMEMBER YOU

I remember you
Making me giggle and
Laugh
When I was upset
With you.
Turned my bad energy
Into good
Bubbling out of me.
Wonder worker.

YOUR OUTGOING LOVE

Your outgoing love toward me
Makes me giggle laugh sing
Play with words feelings
Write love poems
Feel my own silliness bubbling
Both of us in our energy fields
Playing dancing with each other
Loving each other
What a guy
What a guy!

LOVIES

Prissy kisses, sloppy kisses
Wet smackers
Lovies
All kinds of kisses
Love playing in me
Flowing out of me
Making merriness
And peace!

LONGING

Iwishlwishl
Wish
Dearest one could put it in
Thrustingly!

DEAR ONE

Dear one
I may never hold you in my arms again
But I love you so!
Be thankful for what we have had

DOING OUR BEST

The children die and die
Why can't people try
A little harder to save
And heal and bless?

And yet   and yet
I know   I know
That all, at any time
Are doing their best
Hindered from better choices
By their past and genes and raising
By their woundedness
And maybe by their own choices too
And their ignorance

I am the same:
Doing my best
In spite of everything
Wanting so much to better
Things in life
For everyone
Yet just as driven
Blind and ignorant
Caged and limited by
My genes my raising
My woundedness

PEOPLE AND HELL

I feel so sorry for all those
People
In all those old paintings of
People
In Hell.

How hard life is sometimes for
Everyone
Worse for some than
Others

All that eternal painful punishment
People
In agony forever
Maybe only a
Sadist
Could think up all those tortures

Is that really what
We
Think
God
Is?

CAN WE NOT BE WASHED CLEAN

Can we not be washed clean
Of all the hurts and mistakes
Of whatever earth life
We have just been through?

Can't God's dear and wonderful Light
Move through us with release and
    forgetfulness
Forgiveness and understanding?

People are pushed around misunderstood
Taken advantage of
Humiliated
Pressured and forced into
So many situations and behaviors

How can we not understand this and
Have compassion
Instead of threatening eternal
Agony punishment damnation

Are there really any intractable hearts
People unable to quit hurting themselves
And others
Over and over again
Breaking their own hearts
Until they feel nothing
Care nothing about anything

So much hatred of life and maybe
Of themselves
Buried under the character disorder
Under the psychopathic personality
Under the sadistic behavior
Under even all the everyday cruelty
Kindness destroyed over and over
Until it can no longer be found within

Is God so small inadequate not too
Bright, low intelligence
That He/She/It cannot find better ways
To help people?
Who would want such an
    inadequate God?

I have to believe that greater Intelligence
    knows
How to make things right
In each and every one of us
Would never resort to such punishment
Such agony neverending
Such complete shutting out
But I can't bear us hurting us
So deeply anymore
Either

LOVELY DARKNESS

Lovely darkness
That sets me free from daytime's
Noise busyness conflict
Thinkingthingsthrough
Doingness
Thinkingness, relating
I can let go of all that and
Just be
Let my deeper mind run where
It wants

MEDITATION

God is here
So am I
That's enough

THE HEART SINGING

The heart sings hope
The heart sings life
The heart sings happy

JOYOUSNESS UPWELLING

Joyousness upwelling
Upwelling
Like fountains of Light
Holy upwelling swelling uprushing
Joy-rushes
Joy-rushes
Spirit, in me, as me
Joyous One

CENTER

There's the oneness of me at the center
My authenticity integrity
My multivarious selves and beingness
   flow in and out
Of that center
God expressing Itself
Through all forms
Infinitely and joyously
I flow in and out of others' selves and
   they flow in and out of mine
The play of consciousness moving
Toward and away
In and out
Of others and their being
But always coming home to
Center
Integrated self awareness

SOMETIMES

Sometimes it was there
The place where peace is
And goodness and safety

Sometimes it would whisk away
Become a forgotten place
That I couldn't find again for a while
But that was long ago

It seems like I've always known
In this life anyway
How to go into that larger space
Of silence and connectedness
Where goodness and beauty are reality

I think I'm lucky
I found that place so easily
Listening to music
Other ways too
But mostly music

QUIET ROOM

My room is so so quiet
Time stretching
Stretched out infinitely
Slowly

Currents of energy moving
This way and that
Thoughts appearing in my mind
More than memories
Thoughts that lead me to understanding

A great openness within
As if God is looking at everything in me
And I don't mind
Wider and wider open
Freer and freer of everyday limitations
For the moment anyway
Infinite silence and presentness
Together in a timeless slowness

I am myself in my room
And I am somehow with Other
I don't really understand with my mind
But some part of my being knows
And peace expands outward
Wider and wider into everywhere

PRAYING WITHOUT CEASING

You and you and you
All around you must know you
Creatures of the ground and sky
2-legged, 4-legged, 6-legged
And those that fly
Rocks trees ferns oleanders roses jasmine
All must know you
Not by your words or deeds alone
But by your energy field
Your own unique signature

God made us to give and give and give
Praying without ceasing
With our own energy field

And oh, I want to flow out this way
Unceasingly unendingly
No resistance to giving myself

He says:
I will not dwell within another's breast
Nor die to knowing you
Utterly utterly I will sing
And so will you
And every single thing around us all
Intertwined in love but dwelling within self

GENDER

God
Containing all gender
But having no gender
Not He or She
It implying a thing
What pronoun is left to call
God?

CHANGING

Life bursting forth in all directions
And my seamings joining with others'
    seemings
Until I thought
And felt and was anew a freshness
That boded no ill will but only goodness
Through the burgeoning sighing
Breathing that goes on
Underneath the everything of dailyness

BE THANKFUL

Be thankful then dear sweet soulness
For every everydayness light and bright
And groundedness in beingness and
Wonderings of all sorts
And the convoluted meanderings of
    mind and
Oh such heavenly brightness and fiery
    joyous neverendingness
Light within light between light upon
    light
And forgiveness so deep that God's
    neverendingness pours forth
Like richness uncontained unbridled
    fiercely longing
And oh what oh what

MY BROTHER'S DEATH

Let me stay silent and sleepy
Long, and long
I'm not ready now
For such bright hard consciousness
Let me heal my grief
Through silences long
And sleep, through slow days
Meandering and timeless -
When I am ready for more
Awakeness
I'll let you know

I AM ABSORBING DEATH

I am absorbing death
I don't know how I do that
Somewhere down deep inside, the
Process of grieving and gratitude
For another's life
Goes on
Without tears
Deeper than tears and yearning
For another's lost physical presence:
Their smell, their soft skin,
Their ardent life and unknowable depths
Somehow my deep being comes to
   terms
With death and its aftermath

I don't how I absorb death
Only know that I do
And that it is within a quiet place
Taking time and my energy
Something does it for me
Some One does it for me

One of the things I seem to know
Is that my dead ones that I love
Are still with me since I hear them
Speak now and then
Their presence wafts in and out
I am aware of them, and then
Not

Because of this, death seems impossible
To really be a true thing that happens

I know not how I lived and died
I only know down deep inside
That all the things I thought were true
Really are not big enough to contain
All that is

There doesn't seem much more to say
Today and even maybe other days, too
Since the voice comes free of words
And then resumes its speech
Whenever it decides to, or is drawn to
Speak again

I, unknowing, wait to hear what it has
    to say

The final note in a symphony
Comes sometimes first
And then the rest is found
In bits and pieces along the way
Or all at once on an especially quickened
Day of remembrances
That choose form and constancy
That the world might hear and know
Some vital thing that
Music brings to the heart

I am not able yet to be whatever
You wanted me to be in this life, so I
    thought
I know you gave me being, and light
To share with all of the world,

Creatures - salamanders and fish and
cats and even spiders -
But also rocks and moving flashing water
in its glory
And the wide distances of planets and
suns and our earth's body
I know that trees must know me
And the flowering plants around me
The ants in my kitchen that I decided not
to bother when they come to visit

All these must know me
That which sent me here to share my
being with all
Understood that even if I do nothing and
speak nothing
Still must pour out all that I am
To all that is
Always

The love in me clamors to speak
So I must choose, must choose
Simply to listen to whatever comes
I know it is love that wants to speak
To all
Wants to pour itself out into the very
   flow of life and its glory
Wants to, wants to

Did I give enough to you while yet you
Lived here in your body that was familiar
And that I loved?
Did I give enough? I know that I wanted
To give you what I am
Wanted you to know me in my fullness
But also in my narrowness
Faultless and full of faults

Maybe all of life comes here and
Gives unceasingly to all, from us
To that which is around us and all that
Is here in the earth
Somehow that seems to me to be the
Final unending prayer of peace and love

ABOUT THE AUTHOR

Pat has worked as teacher and counselor of children and adults, and as singer and actor in professional opera chorus and filmwork. She taught Dreams and Altered States of Consciousness and led many meditation and dreamwork workshops. Pat began spiritual journeying and writing poetry when she was 14 and is now a senior.

Printed in the United States
By Bookmasters